101 POEMS
TO HELP YOU
UNDERSTAND MEN
(AND WOMEN)

101 POEMS TO HELP YOU UNDERSTAND MEN (AND WOMEN)

EDITED BY

DAISY GOODWIN

HarperCollins*Publishers*

For my father who has always
understood me

HarperCollins*Publishers*
77–85 Fulham Palace Road,
Hammersmith, London w6 8jb
www.fireandwater.com

Published by HarperCollins*Publishers* 2002
9 8 7 6 5 4 3 2 1

Full permissions information may be found on pp. 127–129

A catalogue record for this book
is available from the British Library

ISBN 0-00-713396-0

Set in Postscript Linotype Minion with Optima display
by Rowland Phototypesetting Ltd, Bury St Edmunds, Suffolk

Printed and bound in Great Britain by The Bath Press, Bath

CONTENTS

INTRODUCTION

I am going to be upfront about this: much as I would like to say that I have cracked it, understanding the opposite sex is impossible. It is like living in a foreign country as an adult; you can become fluent in the language, you can steep yourself in the culture, you can know all three verses of the national anthem; but no matter how hard you have worked to assimilate yourself there will always be a joke you don't get, a children's TV star you don't recognise, a word whose inner core of meaning still eludes you. Unless you were born there, you can never wholly belong.

That said, it is worth getting to know the enemy *before* you sleep with him or her. As they say in the army, 'Time spent on reconnaissance is never wasted.' It is called the battle of the sexes for good reason. You wouldn't buy a house without inspecting every room, and yet we make emotional investments *all the time* without ever looking into the cellar. (Of course there are people who would not dream of entering a relationship without a full survey, but I doubt they are the readers of this book.)

Only poets can really go behind enemy lines undetected. So the intelligence collected here is of the very highest order. Bookshops, talkshows and magazines may be full of advice on how to win the next skirmish in the battle of the sexes, but in the end does reading 365 pages on how men evade commitment really enlighten you any more than Byron's couplet from *Don Juan*?

> Man's love is of man's life a thing apart,
> 'Tis woman's whole existence.

So spare yourself the psychobabble and consult the master strategists in the sex war. For no matter how complicated your situation, no matter how pregnant the pauses, a poet will have been there, suffered through it and then written the poem.

This book is arranged by emotional temperature. It starts well back from the front line with the Rules Of Engagement. Read this section with attention and you may never need to place yourself directly in the line of fire. But if you forgot to put on your flak jacket then read the section called Inside The Male Mind, particularly the poem by Philip Larkin called 'Administration', and the What Women Really Want section. It may not yet be too late to retreat with honour.

The middle part of the book is your field guide to unarmed combat – if you want to take possession of the enemy then read the poems under the How To Be Irresistible To The Opposite Sex and Just Say Yes headings. Those of you who have already been occupied by the enemy will take comfort from the Breathless and My Funny Valentine sections, and if the campaign isn't going the way you'd hoped then turn to the poems in the I'm Just Not Ready or even Why Doesn't He Ring, The Bastard? chapters. And for those of you engaged in covert operations, there is plenty of salient advice in the Forbidden Fruit, Married Men and if it is going on longer than it should, Shelf Life sections.

The final parts of the book are for when the battle's lost or won. The victoriously married should read Happy Together; less triumphant unions can turn to For Better Or Worse and You Just Don't Understand. If the whole business has ended in defeat then you will find plenty of fellow sufferers in When Love Congeals and After He's Gone. And for a sense of perspective read Men Have Feelings Too.

I have to admit to a certain amount of bias when compiling this book, I am after all a woman, but I think there are as many poems here for the man who genuinely wants to understand women, as there are for women looking for enlightenment on men. I am just not sure if any man, apart from the occasional poet, really wants to get *too* far inside the female psyche. Women, though, can't *bear* not to know. Read some of the poems by men in this book and you will be one step closer to knowing what goes on in the male mind. But be prepared for the consequences, you may not like it when you get there. As Wendy Cope puts it in 'Defining the Problem':

> I can't forgive you. Even if I could
> You wouldn't pardon me for seeing through you.
> And yet I cannot cure myself of love
> For what I thought you were before I knew you.

I would like to thank so many people who have helped me put this book together: Rashna Nekoo from Talkback, and Kristie Morris for making life possible; Nicola Richardson from the Bridport Bookshop for her suggestions; Mary Enright and the staff at the Poetry Library on the South Bank; Wendy Cope for always seeing the point; my wonderful editor Kate Johnson for smiling through it all; Connie Hallam for her copyright detective work; and above all my sister Tabitha Potts for her brilliant ideas. I should also probably thank all the men who have provided me with research material for this book, and my girlfriends who have helped me dream up the chapter headings. And finally I should thank my husband for not taking it personally, I hope.

101 POEMS
TO HELP YOU
UNDERSTAND MEN
(AND WOMEN)

THE RULES OF ENGAGEMENT

I can say with complete confidence that if you read the following poems closely and follow their advice to the letter *at all times* your love life will move effortlessly into fifth gear. No more carefully contrived 'chance' meetings, or hours spent with friends dissecting the nuances of the message left on the answering machine, or wondering whether the red shoes were after all too obvious. If you can learn to 'drift like a man [or woman] in a mist/ Happy enough to be caught/ Happy to be dismissed', you will find that you will become irresistible to the opposite sex, that scores of them will be hovering over their phones waiting for *you* to ring *them*. The trouble is that those people who are, in Shakespeare's phrase, 'the lords and masters of their faces', are probably born not made. We all know the rules really, but it's like driving when you're drunk: you wouldn't do it if you were sober.

> Man's love is of man's life a thing apart,
>   'Tis woman's whole existence; man may range
> The court, camp, church, the vessel, and the mast;
>   Sword, gown, gain glory, offer in exchange
> Pride, fame, ambition, to fill up his heart,
>   And few there are whom these cannot estrange;
> Men have all these resources, we but one
> To love again, and be again undone.

from *Don Juan*,
Lord Byron

Advice to Lovers

The way to get on with a girl
Is to drift like a man in a mist,
Happy enough to be caught,
Happy to be dismissed.

Glad to be out of her way,
Glad to rejoin her in bed,
Equally grieved or gay
To learn that she's living or dead.

Frank O'Connor

General Review of the Sex Situation

Woman wants monogamy;
Man delights in novelty.
Love is woman's moon and sun;
Man has other forms of fun.
Woman lives but in her lord;
Count to ten, and man is bored.
With this the gist and sum of it,
What earthly good can come of it?

Dorothy Parker

They Loved Each Other

They loved each other, but neither
Would be the first to confess;
Like foes, they gaz'd at each other,
And would die of their love's distress.

Heinrich Heine

50—50

I'm all alone in this world, she said,
Ain't got nobody to share my bed,
Ain't got nobody to hold my hand –
The truth of the matter's
I ain't got no man.

Big Boy opened his mouth and said,
Trouble with you is
You ain't got no head!
If you had a head and used your mind
You could have *me* with you
All the time.

She answered, Babe, what must I do?

He said, Share your bed –
And your money, too.

Langston Hughes

I Am No Good at Love

I am no good at love
My heart should be wise and free
I kill the unfortunate golden goose
Whoever it may be
With over-articulate tenderness
And too much intensity.

I am no good at love
I batter it out of shape
Suspicion tears at my sleepless mind
And, gibbering like an ape,
I lie alone in the endless dark
Knowing there's no escape.

I am no good at love
When my easy heart I yield
Wild words come tumbling from my mouth
Which should have stayed concealed;
And my jealousy turns a bed of bliss
Into a battlefield.

I am no good at love
I betray it with little sins
For I feel the misery of the end
In the moment that it begins
And the bitterness of the last good-bye
Is the bitterness that wins.

Noël Coward

Hotels like Houses

She is the one who takes a shine
to ceilings and to floors,
whose eye finds room for every line
scratched on the wardrobe doors.

She thinks in terms of thick red rope
around the bed, a plaque
above the hardened bathroom soap.
He's always first to pack.

If their affair has awkward spells,
what's bound to cause the rows is
that he treats houses like hotels
and she, hotels like houses.

Sophie Hannah

WHAT WOMEN REALLY WANT

Any man reading these poems looking for the magic bullet will be disappointed, although the 'lineaments of Gratified Desire' isn't a bad place to start. But then prepare to be confused by the poems by Sara Teasdale and Dorothy Parker who like their men in direct proportion to their unavailability (cf. the Rules chapter). If you are the sort of chap who likes to read the instruction manual thoroughly then 'Breakfast' by the Australian poet Chris Mansell is helpfully numbered (although if you are a manual man pay special attention to point 12). I think most women would probably agree with Jennifer Strauss's analysis of what we really want. But don't get complacent because what women say they want and what they really want are not necessarily the same thing at all. It's really for us to know and you to find out . . . Confused? Read the poem by the Aboriginal poet Oodgeroo and count your blessings.

The Question Answer'd

What is it men in women do require?
The lineaments of Gratified Desire.
What is it women do in men require?
The lineaments of Gratified Desire.

William Blake

On Being a Woman

Why is it, when I am in Rome
I'd give an eye to be at home,
But when on native earth I be,
My soul is sick for Italy?

And why with you, my love, my lord,
Am I spectacularly bored,
Yet do you up and leave me – then
I scream to have you back again?

Dorothy Parker

The Look

Stephen kissed me in the spring,
    Robin in the fall,
But Colin only looked at me
    And never kissed at all.

Stephen's kiss was lost in jest,
    Robin's lost in play,
But the kiss in Colin's eyes
    Haunts me night and day.

Sara Teasdale

Breakfast

1
do not cut your hair
a woman likes something
to run her fingers through

2
do not talk about your other women
women do not mind queues
when they're not in them

3
cultivate a manly bum

4
do not pick your nose
too obviously

5
do not be very polite
because she's there

6
forget that you and she are enemies
for the duration

7
do not expect her to believe in you
as Number One Mr Super Hero Incarnate And Flagrante

8
remember that she thinks
the sun can shine out of only one arse at a time
and that this week it's hers

9
when she espouses double standards
do not assume too much
she means you to be faithful

10
do not tell her her skin is soft
when it is not

11
refrain from commenting on her thin arms
as she has refrained from mentioning yours

12
do not fuck by numbers
filling in the little squares
with a touch of red or purple
as the chart suggests

13
finally
leave when you're asked to

14
do not expect breakfast

Chris Mansell

What Women Want

Without in any way wanting
to drop names or big note
the heaviest heavies,
I've news for Freud
and for Pontius Pilate:
even in jest,
they were much too abstract.
Here is something
that women want
specifically, truly:
to lie with a lover
a whole afternoon
so close that the skin
knows boundaries only
by knowing contact
and the mind surrenders
managerial fuss,
until to murmur
'What are you thinking?'
is only a game, words
breaking light
and unimpressive
as the quietest of waves
on tide-washed sand.
It is a truth:
time and desire can stand still
although it is also true
that clocks tick faster
than the light's slow glide

across floor and walls
and that sometimes the tongue
does not touch tenderly
but flares into speech
to set division
sharper than any sword
between sleeping bodies.
Perhaps separation's essential,
like sleep, or like sex,
but women want
sometimes still to lie
truly together
a whole afternoon
awake, without wanting.

Jennifer Strauss

Gifts

'I will bring you love,' said the young lover,
'A glad light to dance in your dark eye.
Pendants I will bring of the white bone,
And gay parrot feathers to deck your hair.'

But she only shook her head.

'I will put a child in your arms,' he said,
'Will be a great headman, great rain-maker.
I will make remembered songs about you
That all the tribes in all the wandering camps
Will sing for ever.'

But she was not impressed.

'I will bring you the still moonlight on the lagoon,
And steal for you the singing of all the birds;
I will bring down the stars of heaven to you,
And put the bright rainbow into your hand.'

'No,' she said, 'bring me tree-grubs.'

Oodgeroo of the Tribe Noonuccal

I'll Have Your Heart

I'll have your heart, if not by gift my knife
Shall carve it out. I'll have your heart, your life.

Stevie Smith

HOW TO BE IRRESISTIBLE TO THE OPPOSITE SEX

If you simply want to fill your address book, then read the Rules section; but if you want to be *adored* then read Margaret Atwood's 'Siren Song' and act accordingly. There is no more potent weapon in the seduction arsenal than to make someone feel that only they can help. But beware, this is strong stuff, so be careful what you wish for. It is much easier to turn them on than to turn them off.

Siren Song

This is the one song everyone
would like to learn: the song
that is irresistible:

the song that forces men
to leap overboard in squadrons
even though they see the beached skulls

the song nobody knows
because anyone who has heard it
is dead, and the others can't remember.

Shall I tell you the secret
and if I do, will you get me
out of this bird suit?

I don't enjoy it here
squatting on this island
looking picturesque and mythical

with these two feathery maniacs,
I don't enjoy singing
this trio, fatal and valuable.

I will tell the secret to you,
to you, only to you.
Come closer. This song

is a cry for help: Help me!
Only you, only you can,
you are unique

at last. Alas
it is a boring song
but it works every time.

Margaret Atwood

INSIDE THE MALE MIND

This section comes with a health warning for women of a sensitive
nature. The default setting of the male mind, as revealed in these poems,
is not for the squeamish. Misogyny has always been with us, the line of
venom here stretches from the ancient Greek poet Palladas right through
to Philip Larkin. But the first rule of engagement is to know your enemy
long before you sleep with them. Read these poems with attention,
particularly the Lawrence poem 'Desire', and you will be prepared for the
worst. And who knows, you may find that poets are prone to exaggeration.
Any man reading these poems and finding himself nodding in agreement
more than once, should give himself up immediately.

Women All Cause Rue

women all
cause rue

but can be nice
on occasional

moments two
to be precise

in bed

& dead

Tony Harrison,
after Palladas

For Anne Gregory

'Never shall a young man,
Thrown into despair
By those great honey-colored
Ramparts at your ear,
Love you for yourself alone
And not for your yellow hair.'

'But I can get a hair-dye
And set such color there,
Brown, or black, or carrot,
That young men in despair
May love me for myself alone
And not for my yellow hair.'

'I heard an old religious man
But yesternight declare
That he had found a text to prove
That only God, my dear,
Could love you for yourself alone
And not for your yellow hair.'

W. B. Yeats

Desire

Ah, in the past, towards rare individuals
I have felt the pull of desire
Oh come, come nearer, come into touch!
Come physically nearer, be flesh to my flesh –

But say little, oh say little,
and afterwards, leave me alone.
Keep your aloneness, leave me my aloneness –
I used to say this, in the past – but now no more.
It has always been a failure.
They have always insisted on love
and on talking about it
and on the me and thee and what we meant to each other.

So now I have no desire any more
Except to be left, in the last resort, alone, quite alone.

D. H. Lawrence

Administration

Day by day your estimation clocks up
Who deserves a smile and who a frown.
And girls you have to tell to pull their socks up
And those whose pants you'd most like to pull down.

Philip Larkin

Clio's

Am I to be blamed for the state of it now? – Surely not –
Her poor wee fractured soul that I loved for its lightness
    and left?
Now she rings up pathetically, not to make claims of me,
Only to be in her wild way solicitous:
'Do you know of a restaurant called *Clio's* – or something
    like that –
At number *forty-three* in its road or street, – and the owner
Is beautiful, rich and Italian – you see, I dreamt of it,
And I can't relax without telling you never to go there,
Divining, somehow, that for you the place is *danger* –'

(But I dine at Clio's every night, poor lamb.)

Mick Imlah

I Never Even Suggested It

I know lots of men who are in love and lots of men who are
    married and lots of men who are both,
And to fall out with their loved ones is what all of them are
    most loth.
They are conciliatory at every opportunity,
Because all they want is serenity and a certain amount of
    impunity.
Yes, many the swain who has finally admitted that the earth
    is flat
Simply to sidestep a spat,
Many the masculine Positively or Absolutely which has been
    diluted to an If
Simply to avert a tiff,
Many the two-fisted executive whose domestic conversation
    is limited to a tactfully interpolated Yes,
And then he is amazed to find that he is being raked
    backwards over a bed of coals nevertheless.
These misguided fellows are under the impression that it
    takes two to make a quarrel, that you can sidestep a crisis
    by nonaggression and nonresistance,
Instead of removing yourself to a discreet distance.
Passivity can be a provoking *modus operandi*;
Consider the Empire and Gandhi.
Silence is golden, but sometimes invisibility is golder.
Because loved ones may not be able to make bricks without
    straw but often they don't need any straw to manufacture
    a bone to pick or blood in their eye or a chip for their soft
    white shoulder.

It is my duty, gentlemen, to inform you that women are
    dictators all, and I recommend to you this moral:
In real life it takes only one to make a quarrel.

Ogden Nash

BLOODY MEN

Read these poems on those days when you want reassurance that the man in your life, while being an insensitive bastard, could quite conceivably be worse. Or, if you are single, read the poem by Anna Akhmatova (incidentally one of my favourite poems) and remember that marriage can be a full stop as well as a beginning. The poems by Sophie Hannah, Maya Angelou and Liz Lochhead are helpful in defining the sort of men you want to avoid. And if it has been a very long dry spell, read 'Bloody Men' by Wendy Cope, and remember, it never rains but it pours, especially if you follow the Rules. It's worth pointing out that while the poems in the previous section write off all women, the poems here with the exception of Wendy Cope's complain about one particular man. They may drive us mad but we don't want to write them *all* off.

Bloody Men

Bloody men are like bloody buses –
You wait for about a year
And as soon as one approaches your stop
Two or three others appear.

You look at them flashing their indicators,
Offering you a ride.
You're trying to read the destinations,
You haven't much time to decide.

If you make a mistake, there is no turning back.
Jump off, and you'll stand there and gaze
While the cars and the taxis and lorries go by
And the minutes, the hours, the days.

Wendy Cope

He Loved Three Things

He loved three things:
White fowls, evensong,
And antique maps of America.

He hated the crying of children,
Raspberry jam at tea,
And female hysteria.

And I was his wife.

Anna Akhmatova,
translated by Jerome Bullitt

Marriage Counsel

Marriage counselor said to me,
'You know your Edgar loves you.
It happens with a man sometimes.
Okay! A few lost days now and then
But he'll be back again.
His heart is home with you!
Trust me!'
I said,
'I know home is where his *heart* is
But damn that!
I wanna be where the rest of him is at.'

Ruby Dee

Slow It Right Down

Nobody gets priority with you
So all concerned must do the best they can:
Be safe and stop, be brave and charge on through –
You are an unmarked crossroads of a man.

Some men I know are double yellow lines
Or traffic lights for everyone to see.
I'm practised when it comes to give way signs
But unmarked crossroads are a mystery

And this time I shall do it by the book,
Slow it right down and read my highway code;
Before reversing, take one final look –
An unmarked crossroads down an unknown road.

Sophie Hannah

Poor Girl

You've got another love
      and I know it
Someone who adores you
      just like me
Hanging on your words
      like they were gold
Thinking that she understands
      your soul
Poor Girl
      Just like me.

You're breaking another heart
      and I know it
And there's nothing
      I can do
If I try to tell her
      what I know
She'll misunderstand
      and make me go
Poor Girl
      Just like me.

You're going to leave her too
       and I know it
She'll never know
       what made you go
She'll cry and wonder
       what went wrong
Then she'll begin
       to sing this song
Poor Girl
       Just like me.

Maya Angelou

Cowboys and Priests

The lady said men could be divided
Into cowboys and priests
But she was not so hot at spotting
The difference between men and beasts.
She was prone to such confusion
It twisted her in knots –
She said mark well, you just can't tell
A leopard by its spots.
Yet they said men could be divided
Into cowboys and priests.

Oh, after their devotions
He'd prayed to be released
When he looked beyond her
To the wide blue yonder
Was he cowboy then, or priest?
Oh, she was tired and had taken to declining
All invitations to feasts
Due to the confusion
Between cowboys and priests.

She said along would come some cowboy
When your whole soul cried for a priest
She was tired of being surprised by a wind from the west
When her weathercock pointed east.
Oh, he'd want to hear her confession
And to leave her feeling blessed
So she'd see a sheep in wolf's clothing
As all her love went west.
Yes every man can be divided
Part cowboy, part priest.

Liz Lochhead

MEN HAVE FEELINGS TOO

I thought it was important at this point in the book to be reminded that it isn't always their fault, in fact there are times when you could feel almost sorry for them. Who could read Yeats's poem 'The Folly of Being Comforted' without a twinge of recognition? Heartbreak and anguish are genderless. The difference between male and female heartbreak is that while men project their misery onto the female sex as a whole, read the Hugo Williams and the Pushkin poems and you will see what I mean, women tend to blame themselves – the After He's Gone section has ample evidence of this. So don't worry too much if you break a man's heart, he'll know it wasn't his fault.

Girl

From the crowded platform
Of this end-of-line resort
You wave goodbye to me.

There are tears in your eyes
As you scan the new arrivals
For your next lover.

Hugo Williams

The Folly of Being Comforted

One that is ever kind said yesterday:
'Your well-beloved's hair has threads of grey,
And little shadows come about her eyes;
Time can but make it easier to be wise
Though now it seems impossible, and so
All that you need is patience.'

Heart cries, 'No,

I have not a crumb of comfort, not a grain.
Time can but make her beauty over again:
Because of that great nobleness of hers
The fire that stirs about her, when she stirs,
Burns but more clearly. O she had not these ways
When all the wild summer was in her gaze.'

O heart! O heart! if she'd but turn her head,
You'd know the folly of being comforted.

W. B. Yeats

She's Gazing at You So Tenderly

She's gazing at you so tenderly.
Drowning you in sparkling conversation,
Gay and witty, and her eyes
Absorbing you with their yearning.
But last night she was using all her skill
To give me secretly her little foot
Under the tablecloth for me to caress.

Alexander Pushkin

Like the Touch of Rain

Like the touch of rain she was
On a man's flesh and hair and eyes
When the joy of waking thus
Has taken him by surprise:

With the love of the storm he burns,
He sings, he laughs, well I know how,
But forgets when he returns
As I shall not forget her 'Go now'.

Those two words shut a door
Between me and the blessed rain
That was never shut before
And will not open again.

Edward Thomas

Late Last Night

Late last night I
Set on my steps and cried.
Wasn't nobody gone,
Neither had nobody died.

I was cryin'
Cause you broke my heart in two.
You looked at me cross-eyed
And broke my heart in two –

So I was cryin'
On account of
You!

Langston Hughes

BELOW THE BELT

I suppose there are some men who might find the association that Sharon Olds draws between the male member and the slug disturbing, but I think it is charmingly erotic. I include Robert Mezey's poem about what men dream of as the 'perfect end to a long day's hunt', to even the score a little.

The Connoisseuse of Slugs

When I was a connoisseuse of slugs
I would part the ivy leaves, and look for the
naked jelly of those gold bodies,
translucent strangers glistening along the
stones, slowly, their gelatinous bodies
at my mercy. Made mostly of water, they would shrivel
to nothing if they were sprinkled with salt,
but I was not interested in that. What I liked
was to draw aside the ivy, breathe the
odor of the wall, and stand there in silence
until the slug forgot I was there
and sent its antennae up out of its
head, the glimmering umber horns
rising like telescopes, until finally the
sensitive knobs would pop out the ends,
delicate and intimate. Years later,
when I first saw a naked man,

I gasped with pleasure to see that quiet
mystery reenacted, the slow
elegant being coming out of hiding and
gleaming in the dark air, eager and so
trusting you could weep.

Sharon Olds

Balls

Actually: it's the balls I look for, always.
Men in the street, offices, cars, restaurants.
it's the nuts I imagine –
firm, soft, in hairy sacks
the way they are
down there rigged between the thighs,
the funny way they are.
One in front, a little in front of the other,
slightly higher. The way they slip
between your fingers, the way they
slip around in their soft sack.
The way they swing when he walks,
hang down when he bends
over. You see them sometimes bright pink
out of a pair of shorts
when he sits wide and unaware,
the hair sparse and wiry
like that on a poland china pig.
You can see the skin right through – speckled,
with wrinkles like a prune, but loose,
slipping over those kernels
rocking the smooth, small huevos.
So delicate, the cock becomes a diversion,
a masthead overlarge, its flag distracting
from beautiful pebbles beneath.

Anne McNaughton

A Thousand Chinese Dinners

From a thousand Chinese dinners, one cookie:
Good fortune in love, also a better position.

So much for both. Too many humorless people
Who can't believe that God could have made the cunt.

Maybe he didn't make it. Maybe hydrogen
Made nitrogen and one thing led to another.

Some hold that early man stumbled upon it
While dreaming of the perfect end to a long day's hunt.

But I say only Italians, with their flavor for drama,
Could have invented this fragrant envelope.

Let's drink to the Italians, especially Catullus,
Who knew it was no joke but couldn't help laughing.

Robert Mezey

MARRIED MEN

A recent survey on fidelity found that 81% of married men having affairs described themselves as 'extremely happy' as opposed to only 32% of women in the same situation. This chilling statistic is worth bearing in mind the next time you are tempted by the unavailable. But if it's too late and you have become the oblique angle in someone else's marriage, then you may find some consolation in the poems here. Maya Angelou is, as always, on the money in her poem 'They Went Home', you are kidding yourself if you think any different. (And if you are still waiting for him to leave her, turn to the Shelf Life section ASAP.) I like the way that Anne Sexton's poem acknowledges the unspoken but intense connection between the mistress and the wife, and 'I am a watercolor/ I wash off' is the most graceful of exit lines. And for the 19% of married men who have problems with the having their cake and eating it concept I have included the Felix Pollak poem.

For My Lover, Returning to His Wife

She has always been there, my darling.
She is, in fact, exquisite.
Fireworks in the dull middle of February
and as real as a cast-iron pot.

Let's face it, I have been momentary.
A luxury. A bright red sloop in the harbor.
My hair rising like smoke from the car window.
Littleneck clams out of season.

She is more than that. She is your have to have,
has grown you your practical, your tropical growth.
This is not an experiment. She is all harmony.
She sees to oars and oarlocks for the dinghy,

I give you back your heart.
I give you permission –

She is so naked and singular.
She is the sum of yourself and your dream.
Climb her like a monument, step after step.
She is solid.

As for me, I am a watercolor.
I wash off.

Anne Sexton

They Went Home

They went home and told their wives,
      that never once in all their lives,
      had they known a girl like me,
But . . . They went home.

They said my house was licking clean,
      no word I spoke was ever mean,
      I had an air of mystery,
But . . . They went home.

My praises were on all men's lips,
      they liked my smile, my wit, my hips,
      they'd spend one night, or two or three.
But . . .

Maya Angelou

The Dream

He dreamed of
an open window.
A vagina, said
his psychiatrist.
Your divorce, said
his mistress.
Suicide, said
an ominous voice within him.
It means you should close the window
or you'll catch cold, said
his mother.
His wife said
nothing.
He dared not tell her
such a
dangerous dream.

Felix Pollak

A real husband always is suspicious,
    But still no less suspects in the wrong place.
Jealous of some one who had no such wishes,
    Or pandering blindly to his own disgrace,
By harbouring some dear friend extremely vicious;
    The last indeed's infallibly the case:
And when the spouse and friend are gone off wholly,
He wonders at their vice, and not his folly.

from *Don Juan,*
Lord Byron

FORBIDDEN FRUIT

You know, of course, that it is a bad idea, that it is bound to end in tears, that everything you say and do will be the stuff of cliché; but the hot searchlight of attention makes the real life, everyday stuff seem like fairy lights. Read the Rosemary Tonks poem if you are thinking that you can keep it all compartmentalised in tidy boxes: there are some men, and the French, who can keep things confined on a kind of *cinq à sept* basis, but for most of us adultery can't help battering through the walls and taking over the whole of our lives – and it *does* always end in tears. Apparently scientists (married ones I bet) have just isolated a gene which they believe causes infidelity. So don't blame yourself, blame your DNA; I am sure your spouse will understand.

Story of a Hotel Room

Thinking we were safe – insanity!
We went to make love. All the same
Idiots to trust the little hotel bedroom.
Then in the gloom . . .
. . . And who does not know that pair of shutters
With the awkward hook on them
All screeching whispers? Very well then, in the gloom
We set about acquiring one another
Urgently! But on a temporary basis
Only as guests – just guests of one another's senses.

But idiots to feel so safe you hold back nothing
Because the bed of cold, electric linen
Happens to be illicit . . .
To make love as well as that is ruinous.

Londoner, Parisian, someone should have warned us
That without permanent intentions
You have absolutely no protection
– If the act is clean, authentic, sumptuous,
The concurring deep love of the heart
Follows the naked work, profoundly moved by it.

Rosemary Tonks

At 3 a.m.

the room contains no sound
except the ticking of the clock
which has begun to panic
like an insect, trapped
in an enormous box.

Books lie open on the carpet.

Somewhere else
you're sleeping
and beside you there's a woman
who is crying quietly
so you won't wake.

Wendy Cope

And love hung still as crystal over the bed
    And filled the corners of the enormous room;
The boom of dawn that left her sleeping, showing
    The flowers mirrored in the mahogany table.

O my love, if only I were able
    To protract this hour of quiet after passion,
Not ration happiness but keep this door for ever
    Closed on the world, its own world closed within it.

But dawn's waves trouble with the bubbling minute,
    The names of books come clear upon their shelves,
The reason delves for duty and you will wake
    With a start and go on living on your own.

The first train passes and the windows groan,
    Voices will hector and your voice become
A drum in tune with theirs, which all last night
    Like sap that fingered through a hungry tree
Asserted our one night's identity.

from *Trilogy for X*
Louis MacNeice

'Tis a sad thing, I cannot choose but say,
    And all the fault of that indecent sun,
Who cannot leave alone our helpless clay,
    But will keep baking, broiling, burning on,
That howsoever people fast and pray,
    The flesh is frail, and so the soul undone:
What men call gallantry, and gods adultery,
Is much more common where the climate's sultry.

from *Don Juan,*
Lord Byron

SHELF LIFE

The most unromantic piece of advice I have ever received was from a married male poet notorious for his complicated love life, 'the best time to get married is in your twenties, you are at the peak of your physical attractiveness, there is plenty of choice, and nobody's perfect'. A horribly pragmatic male point of view, but one that some of my still single, thirty-something friends are beginning to have sympathy with. But despite my slightly gloomy preamble, I am a great believer in the watched kettle theory of love: the moment you start getting really involved in something that would make a love affair impossible, you will meet THE ONE. But if the waiting is getting to you, read the Maya Angelou poem, it is never too late.

Advice to Young Women

When you're a spinster of forty,
You're reduced to considering bids
From husbands inclined to be naughty
And divorcés obsessed with their kids.

So perhaps you should wed in a hurry,
But that has its drawbacks as well.
The answer? There's no need to worry –
Whatever you do, life is hell.

Wendy Cope

I Used to Tell You

I used to tell you, 'Frances, we grow old.
The years fly away. Don't be so private
With those parts. A chaste maid is an old maid.'
Unnoticed by your disdain, old age crept
Close to us. Those days are gone past recall.
And now you come, penitent and crying
Over your old lack of courage, over
Your present lack of beauty. It's all right.
Closed in your arms, we'll share our smashed delights.
I forgive and take now. It's what I wanted,
If not what I want.

Ausonius,
translated by Kenneth Rexroth

Seven Women's Blessed Assurance

1

One thing about me,
I'm little and low,
find me a man
wherever I go.

2

They call me string bean
'cause I'm so tall.
Men see me,
they ready to fall.

3

I'm young as morning
and fresh as dew.
Everybody loves me
and so do you.

4

I'm fat as butter
and sweet as cake.
Men start to tremble
each time I shake.

5

I'm little and lean,
sweet to the bone.
They like to pick me up
and carry me home.

6
When I passed forty
I dropped pretense,
'cause men like women
who got some sense.

7
Fifty-five is perfect,
so is fifty-nine,
'cause every man needs
to rest sometime.

Maya Angelou

Chat Show

'You never married.' 'No,' he said,
'Relationships were not my *forte*.'
'Any regrets?' 'Ah . . .' Here we supply
the bitter-sweet accompaniment.
Of course. But he had higher ends
than procreation. Who could fill
the deep well of his genius? 'Perhaps.'

'You never married.' 'No,' she said,
'I wasn't asked.' Poor thing,
ceaselessly shovelling her work
into that lack. 'Regrets?'
'No, none at all.' Oh well, she would say that.

Vicki Raymond

I'M JUST NOT READY

'I really like you, and I love being with you, but I'm just not ready to settle down yet.' You know perfectly well that the only response to this kind of talk is to leave immediately (look at the Shelf Life section for the reasons why), but somehow you find yourself hanging in there, not realising that 'I'm just not ready' is code for 'I am making do with you, until something better comes along.' If you do leave, you will be amazed at how quickly the embossed invitation to your ex's wedding lands on your doormat. So read these poems and get the next flight out.

Ballade at Thirty-Five

This, no song of an ingénue,
   This, no ballad of innocence;
This, the rhyme of a lady who
   Followed ever her natural bents.
   This, a solo of sapience,
This, a chantey of sophistry,
   This, the sum of experiments –
I loved them until they loved me.

Decked in garments of sable hue,
   Daubed with ashes of myriad Lents,
Wearing shower bouquets of rue,
   Walk I ever in penitence.
   Oft I roam, as my heart repents,
Through God's acre of memory,
   Marking stones, in my reverence,
'I loved them until they loved me.'

Pictures pass me in long review –
   Marching columns of dead events.
I was tender and, often, true;
   Ever a prey to coincidence.
   Always knew I the consequence;
Always saw what the end would be.
   We're as Nature has made us – hence
I loved them until they loved me.

Dorothy Parker

The Libertine

In the old days with married women's stockings
Twisted round his bedpost he felt himself a gay
Dog but now his liver has begun to groan,
Now that pick-ups are the order of the day:
O leave me easy, leave me alone.

Voluptuary in his 'teens and cynic in his twenties,
He ran through women like a child through growing hay
Looking for a lost toy whose capture might atone
For his own guilt and the cosmic disarray:
O leave me easy, leave me alone.

He never found the toy and has forgotten the faces,
Only remembers the props . . . a scent-spray
Beside the bed or a milk-white telephone
Or through the triple ninon the acrid trickle of day:
O leave me easy, leave me alone.

Long fingers over the gunwale, hair in a hair-net,
Furs in January, cartwheel hats in May,
And after the event the wish to be alone –
Angels, goddesses, bitches, all have edged away:
O leave me easy, leave me alone.

So now, in middle age, his erotic programme
Torn in two, if after such a delay
An accident should offer him his own
Fulfilment in a woman, still he would say:
O leave me easy, leave me alone.

Louis MacNeice

One Two Three

One two three four five six seven eight
    Marry your girl before it's too late.
Do not reflect, do not delay,
    Or someone else will snatch her away.
Then I had honey, and did not eat,
    And another came and found it sweet.
There were two sisters – one was fair,
    The second was dark, and dark her hair.
They were both lovely and good to see,
    And I loved them both equally.
I pondered and pondered with aching head.
    I couldn't decide which to wed.
Months passed and still I could not see
    Which I should ask my wife to be.
Alas two devils came one day,
    And carried both of them away.
Now I am old and sick and worn,
    Broken-hearted and forlorn.
And I say to all who will listen to me,
    Don't let your lives like my life be.
One two three four five six seven eight
    Marry your girl before it's too late.
Do not reflect, do not delay,
    Don't let another snatch her away.

Anon, Hebrew poem

WOMEN BEHAVING BADLY

I think that in the quest to understand men, it is important to remember that in Kipling's phrase, 'the female of the species is more deadly than the male'. Sometimes the only way to behave is badly: Anna Wickham's poem 'The Fired Pot' sets out the reasons. I love the Edna St Vincent Millay poem that ends 'Some sane day, not too bright and not too stormy/ I shall be gone, and you may whistle for me.' There is nothing like knowing where the exit is to keep a relationship vivid. The Robert Frost poem should be read by anyone who is spending too much time at the office; you don't want to come back to find there's nobody home.

The Impulse

It was too lonely for her there,
   And too wild,
And since there were but two of them,
   And no child.

And work was little in the house,
   She was free,
And followed where he furrowed field,
   Or felled tree.

She rested on a log and tossed
   The fresh chips,
With a song only to herself
   On her lips.

And once she went to break a bough
   Of black alder.
She strayed so far she scarcely heard
   When he called her –

And didn't answer – didn't speak –
   Or return.
She stood, and she ran and hid
   In the fern.

He never found her, though he looked
   Everywhere,
And he asked at her mother's house
   Was she there.

Sudden and swift and light as that
   The ties gave,
And he learned of finalities
   Besides the grave.

Robert Frost

The Fired Pot

In our town, people live in rows.
The only irregular thing in a street is the steeple;
And where that points to God only knows,
And not the poor disciplined people!

And I have watched the women growing old,
Passionate about pins, and pence, and soap,
Till the heart within my wedded breast grew cold,
And I lost hope.

But a young soldier came to our town,
He spoke his mind most candidly.
He asked me quickly to lie down,
And that was very good for me.

For though I gave him no embrace –
Remembering my duty –
He altered the expression of my face,
And gave me back my beauty.

Anna Wickham

Mississippi Winter IV

My father and mother both
used to warn me
that 'a whistling woman and a crowing
hen would surely come to
no good end.' And perhaps I should
have listened to them.
But even at the time I knew
that though my end probably might
not
be good
I must whistle
like a woman undaunted
until I reached it.

Alice Walker

Sonnet to Gath

Oh, oh, you will be sorry for that word!
Give back my book and take my kiss instead.
Was it my enemy or my friend I heard,
'What a big book for a such little head!'
Come, I will show you now my newest hat,
And you may watch me purse my mouth and prink!
Oh, I shall love you still, and all of that.
I never again shall tell you what I think.
I shall be sweet and crafty, soft and sly;
You will not catch me reading any more:
I shall be called a wife to pattern by;
And some day when you knock and push the door,
Some sane day, not too bright and not too stormy,
I shall be gone, and you may whistle for me.

Edna St Vincent Millay

Excavations

Here is a hole full of men shouting
'I don't love you. I loved you once
but I don't now. I went off you,
or I was frightened, or my wife was pregnant,
or I found I preferred men instead.'

What can I say to that kind of talk?
'Thank you for being honest, you
who were so shifty when it happened,
pretending you were suddenly busy
with your new job or your new conscience.'

I chuck them a shovelful of earth
to make them blink for a bit, to smirch
their green eyes and their long lashes
or their brown eyes . . . Pretty bastards:
the rain will wash their bawling faces

and I bear them little enough ill will.
Now on to the next hole,
covered and fairly well stamped down,
full of the men whom I stopped loving
and didn't always tell at the time –

being, I found, rather busy
with my new man or my new freedom.
These are quiet and unaccusing,
cuddled up with their subsequent ladies,
hardly unsettling the bumpy ground.

Fleur Adcock

JUST SAY YES

You could follow the Rules in which case just skip this section and know you've done the right, if rather boring thing, or you could just say yes; as Andrew Marvell points out, 'The grave's a fine and private place/ But none, I think, do there embrace.' If life really is boredom and then fear, then you might as well go for it. The Maya Angelou poem is there to show that women can seduce as urgently as men.

Come. And Be My Baby

The highway is full of big cars
going nowhere fast
And folks is smoking anything that'll burn
Some people wrap their lives around a cocktail glass
And you sit wondering
where you're going to turn.
I got it.
Come. And be my baby.

Some prophets say the world is gonna end tomorrow
But others say we've got a week or two
The paper is full of every kind of blooming horror
And you sit wondering
What you're gonna do.
I got it.
Come. And be my baby.

Maya Angelou

To His Coy Mistress

Had we but world enough, and time,
This coyness, Lady, were no crime.
We would sit down and think which way
To walk and pass our long love's day.
Thou by the Indian Ganges' side
Shouldst rubies find: I by the tide
Of Humber would complain. I would
Love you ten years before the Flood,
And you should, if you please, refuse
Till the conversion of the Jews.
My vegetable love should grow
Vaster than empires, and more slow;
An hundred years should go to praise
Thine eyes and on thy forehead gaze;
Two hundred to adore each breast;
But thirty thousand to the rest;
An age at least to every part,
And the last age should show your heart;
For, Lady, you deserve this state,
Nor would I love at lower rate.

But at my back I always hear
Time's winged chariot hurrying near;
And yonder all before us lie
Deserts of vast eternity.
Thy beauty shall no more be found,
Nor, in thy marble vault, shall sound
My echoing song: then worms shall try
That long preserved virginity,

And your quaint honour turn to dust,
And into ashes all my lust:
The grave's a fine and private place,
But none, I think, do there embrace.

    Now therefore, while the youthful hue
Sits on thy skin like morning dew,
And while thy willing soul transpires
At every pore with instant fires,
Now let us sport us while we may,
And now, like amorous birds of prey,
Rather at once our time devour
Than languish in his slow-chapt power.
Let us roll all our strength and all
Our sweetness up into one ball,
And tear our pleasures with rough strife
Through the iron gates of life:
Thus, though we cannot make our sun
Stand still, yet we will make him run.

Andrew Marvell

You'll Love Me Yet

You'll love me yet! – and I can tarry
    Your love's protracted growing:
June rear'd that bunch of flowers you carry,
    From seeds of April's sowing.

I plant a heartful now: some seed
    At least is sure to strike,
And yield – what you'll not pluck indeed,
    Not love, but, may be, like.

You'll look at least on love's remains,
    A grave's one violet:
Your look? – that pays a thousand pains.
    What's death? You'll love me yet!

Robert Browning

WHY DOESN'T HE RING, THE BASTARD?

I suppose men wait by the telephone too, but not so religiously and not with such masochistic relish. They have after all got other things to do. The only remedy to telephone torture is to become so elusive yourself that getting hold of you becomes a challenge rather than a duty, but if you were that kind of person you wouldn't be reading this. So all I can advise is to read the poems here and go out with your mobile switched off. If he really wants to talk to you, he'll ring back later.

Going Too Far

Cuddling the new telephone directory
After I found your name in it
Was going too far.

It's a safe bet you're not hugging a phone book,
Wherever you are.

Wendy Cope

Telephone Song

Hi there, thought I would call you
(Why Why did I pick up the telephone)
I'm fine just wondring . . . how are you
(Swore blind not to touch the telephone)

I've nothing new to say
Things've been OK
With me
Without you

Last time I phoned
You were not alone
Love lost lines crossed
Should have known

Midnight your time, six a.m. mine
All night trying to reach you
Time is up and I'm all strung up and we're too
Hung up to hang up the telephone

Why why did I call you up
(Can't touch you on the telephone)
Long distance loving's got to stop
Cut off by the telephone.

Liz Lochhead

BREATHLESS

I have read, and sometimes I even believe, that falling in love is all about making a narcissistic object choice; subconsciously you project an aspect of your personality on someone else's wide screen and proceed to find it irresistible. I have also heard that falling in love is a chemical process akin to heroin addiction: once your brain is flooded with those feel good endorphins, there's no going back, you are always going to want more. What's interesting about these rationalisations of love is that their basic premise is something that poets have always known: that falling in love is quite involuntary. As Elizabeth Bishop puts it: 'Love's the boy stood on the burning deck/ trying to recite "The boy stood on/ the burning deck" . . .' If you're currently in love you will find the poems here perfect mood music, but if you are not afflicted at the moment or worse still recently out of love, then save these for later. One day, believe it or not, you will need them.

On Love

Love's thrice a robber, however you take it:
He's desperate,

        sleepless,

                and he strips us naked.

Diophanes of Myrina,
translated by Dudley Fitts

Casabianca

Love's the boy stood on the burning deck
trying to recite 'The boy stood on
the burning deck.' Love's the son
    stood stammering elocution
    while the poor ship in flames went down.

Love's the obstinate boy, the ship,
even the swimming sailors, who
would like a schoolroom platform, too.

Elizabeth Bishop

Gloire de Dijon

When she rises in the morning
I linger to watch her;
She spreads the bath-cloth underneath the window
And the sunbeams catch her
Glistening white on the shoulders,
While down her sides the mellow
Golden shadow glows as
She stoops to the sponge, and her swung breasts
Sway like full-blown yellow
Gloire de Dijon roses.

She drips herself with water, and her shoulders
Glisten as silver, they crumple up
Like wet and falling roses, and I listen
For the sluicing of their rain-dishevelled petals.
In the window full of sunlight
Concentrates her golden shadow
Fold on fold, until it glows as
Mellow as the glory roses.

D. H. Lawrence

The Good-morrow

I wonder by my troth, what thou, and I
Did, till we lov'd? were we not wean'd till then?
But suck'd on countrey pleasures, childishly?
Or snorted we in the seven sleepers den?
'Twas so; But this, all pleasures fancies bee.
If ever any beauty I did see,
Which I desir'd, and got, 'twas but a dreame of thee.

And now good morrow to our waking soules,
Which watch not one another out of feare;
For love, all love of other sights controules,
And makes one little roome, and every where.
Let sea-discoverers to new worlds have gone,
Let maps to others, worlds on worlds have showne,
Let us possesse one world, each hath one, and is one.

My face in thine eye, thine in mine appeares,
And true plaine hearts doe in the faces rest,
Where can we finde two better hemispheares
Without sharpe North, without declining West?
Whatever dies, was not mixt equally;
If our two loves be one, or, thou and I
Love so alike, that none doe slacken, none can die.

John Donne

Gray Room

Although you sit in a room that is gray,
Except for the silver
Of the straw-paper,
And pick
At your pale white gown;
Or lift one of the green beads
Of your necklace.
To let it fall;
Or gaze at your green fan
Printed with the red branches of a red willow;
Or, with one finger,
Move the leaf in the bowl –
The leaf that has fallen from the branches of the forsythia
Beside you . . .
What is all this?
I know how furiously your heart is beating.

Wallace Stevens

O Best of All Nights,
Return and Return Again

How she let her long hair down over her shoulders, making
    a love cave around her face. Return and return again.
How when the lamplight was lowered she pressed against
    him, twining her fingers in his. Return and return
    again.
How their legs swam together like dolphins and their toes
    played like little tunnies. Return and return again.
How she sat beside him cross-legged, telling him stories of
    her childhood. Return and return again.
How she closed her eyes when his were open, how they
    breathed together, breathing each other. Return and
    return again.
How they fell into slumber, their bodies curled together
    like two spoons. Return and return again.
How they went together to Otherwhere, the fairest land
    they had ever seen. Return and return again.
O best of all nights, return and return again.

James Laughlin,
after the *Pervigilum Veneris* and
Propertius's *Nox miki candida*

83

MY FUNNY VALENTINE

Even the most sorted woman has days when she thinks that if she lost 10lbs, had blonde curls, thinner ankles or had worn more sunscreen when she was younger, then all her romantic difficulties would evaporate. I include these poems to remind you that he fell for the way you are now, not for the person you would quite like to be some day. As someone with two left feet, I particularly like the 'Love Poem' by John Frederick Nims.

Love Poem

My clumsiest dear, whose hands shipwreck vases,
At whose quick touch all glasses chip and ring,
Whose palms are bulls in china, burs in linen,
And have no cunning with any soft thing

Except all ill-at-ease fidgeting people:
The refugee uncertain at the door
You make at home; deftly you steady
The drunk clambering on his undulant floor.

Unpredictable dear, the taxi drivers' terror,
Shrinking from far headlights pale as a dime
Yet leaping before red apoplectic streetcars –
Misfit in any space. And never on time.

A wrench in clocks and the solar system. Only
With words and people and love you move at ease.
In traffic of wit expertly manoeuvre
And keep us, all devotion, at your knees.

Forgetting your coffee spreading on our flannel,
Your lipstick grinning on our coat,
So gayly in love's unbreakable heaven
Our souls on glory of spilt bourbon float.

Be with me, darling, early and late. Smash glasses –
I will study wry music for your sake.
For should your hands drop white and empty
All the toys of the world would break.

John Frederick Nims

No Loathsomeness in Love

What I fancy, I approve,
No dislike there is in love:
Be my Mistress short or tall,
And distorted therewithal:
Be she likewise one of those,
That an acre hath of nose:
Be her forehead, and her eyes
Full of incongruities:
Be her cheeks so shallow too,
As to shew her tongue wag through:
Be her lips ill hung, or set,
And her grinders black as jet;
Has she thin hair, hath she none,
She's to me a paragon.

Robert Herrick

WHATEVER YOU WANT

If you follow the advice in the Rules section, you will definitely not have your dreams treated like a doormat, because you will be the one trampling their fantasies. But once in a while everyone should be in Auden's phrase 'the more loving one'. The kind of people who let their answering machine pick up on principle don't know what they are missing.

Tell me right away if I'm disturbing you,
he said as he stepped inside my door,
and I'll leave at once.

You not only disturb me, I said,
you shatter my entire existence.
Welcome.

Eeva Kilpi

Aedh Wishes for the Cloths of Heaven

Had I the heavens' embroidered cloths,
Enwrought with golden and silver light,
The blue and the dim and the dark cloths
Of night and light and the half light,
I would spread the cloths under your feet:
But I, being poor, have only my dreams;
I have spread my dreams under your feet;
Tread softly because you tread on my dreams.

W. B. Yeats

She Tells Her Love
While Half Asleep

She tells her love while half asleep,
   In the dark hours,
      With half-words whispered low:
As Earth stirs in her winter sleep
   And puts out grass and flowers
      Despite the snow,
      Despite the falling snow.

Robert Graves

YOU'RE BLOCKING MY VIEW

'Mmm, that feels really nice, but would you mind shifting to the left a bit, I just want to see what the score is.' Any woman who has ever felt unable to compete with eleven men, will have their deepest fears confirmed by Glyn Maxwell's poem 'The Perfect Match' which ends with the lines, 'Love's one thing, but this is the Big Chief.' In the interests of fairness I did try and find a poem by a woman comparing men unfavourably to shopping as a recreation, but I couldn't find one.

The Perfect Match

There is nothing like the five minutes to go:
Your lads one up, your lads one down, or the whole
    Thing even. How you actually feel,
        What you truly know,
Is that your lads are going to do it. So,

However many times in the past the fact
Is that they didn't, however you screamed and strained,
    Pummelled the floor, looked up and groaned
        As the Seiko ticked
On, when the ultimate ball is nodded or kicked.

The man in the air is you. Your beautiful wife
May curl in the corner yawningly calm and true,
    But something's going on with you
        That lasts male life.
Love's one thing, but this is the Big Chief.

Glyn Maxwell

Poem

If the night flights keep you awake
I will call London Airport and tell them
to land their dangerous junk elsewhere.

And if you fall asleep with the sleeve
of my jacket under your head,
sooner than wake you, I'll cut it off.

But if you say:
'Fix me a plug on this mixer',
I grumble and take my time.

Christopher Logue

Timekeeping

Late home for supper,
He mustn't seem drunk.
'The pob cluck', he begins,
And knows he is sunk.

Wendy Cope

HAPPY TOGETHER

These are the poems to read if you are beginning to lose heart either in the opposite sex in general or in one example of it in particular. There *are* happy endings out there. And it really helps if both parties follow Ogden Nash's advice in 'A Word to Husbands'.

A Word to Husbands

To keep your marriage brimming,
With love in the loving cup,
Whenever you're wrong, admit it;
Whenever you're right, shut up.

Ogden Nash

Metropolitan

The city's manic, but my Love is sane.
He likes the hustle – doesn't want to move.
My Love's not only urban, but urbane.

I'd leave tomorrow – gladly pack it in,
but he prefers the lamplight to the stars.
We lie in bed marooned inside the din.

He has to stay in reach of Waterloo.
He has to travel in the outside lane.
I tell him that I've grown to like it too.
That's love. You stack the loss against the gain.

Connie Bensley

To My Dear and Loving Husband

If ever two were one, then surely we.
If ever man were loved by wife, then thee;
If ever wife was happy in a man,
Compare with me, ye women, if you can.
I prize thy love more than whole mines of gold
Or all the riches that the East doth hold.
My love is such that rivers cannot quench,
Nor ought but love from thee, give recompense.
Thy love is such I can no way repay,
The heavens reward thee manifold, I pray.
Then while we live, in love let's so persevere
That when we live no more, we may live ever.

Anne Bradstreet

Fireworks Poem

Write it in fire across the night:
Some men are more or less all right.

Wendy Cope

The Marriage

They will fit, she thinks,
but only if her backbone
cuts exactly into his rib cage,
and only if his knees
dock exactly under her knees
and all four
agree on a common angle.

All would be well
if only
they could face each other.

Even as it is
there are compensations
for having to meet
nose to neck
chest to scapula
groin to rump
when they sleep.

They look, at least,
as if they were going
in the same direction.

Anne Stevenson

This to the Crown, and blessing of my life,
The much lov'd husband, of a happy wife.
To him, whose constant passion found the art
To win a stubborn, and ungrateful heart;
And to the World, by tend'rest proof discovers
They err, who say that husbands can't be lovers.

from 'A Letter to Daphnis, April 2nd 1685',
Anne Finch, Countess of Winchilsea

FOR BETTER OR WORSE

If the poems in the previous section have made you feel newly optimistic then you should definitely skip this bit until the next time you start wondering about undetectable poisons. 'Talking in Bed' by Philip Larkin is beautiful but has to be possibly the bleakest poem about human relationships ever written. As the American poet Diane Thiel points out in 'Bedside Readers', '– unless you want a timely end/ Don't read your lover "Talking in Bed" in bed.' I had to read 'Infidelities' by Moyra Donaldson a couple of times before I got the full extent of the duplicity involved. I'd say it was essential reading for anyone who thinks they are safe because their partner would never have the gumption to stray.

A Wife

So much did I love my wife before we tied the knot
That I could have eaten her up right on the spot;
Now when the days go by without even a kiss,
I regret most sincerely that I had not done this.

Anon, Polish poem

Her back turned
the husband zaps his wife
with the TV remote.

Katrina Middleton

Talking in Bed

Talking in bed ought to be easiest,
Lying together there goes back so far,
An emblem of two people being honest.

Yet more and more time passes silently.
Outside, the wind's incomplete unrest
Builds and disperses clouds about the sky,

And dark towns heap up on the horizon.
None of this cares for us. Nothing shows why
At this unique distance from isolation

It becomes still more difficult to find
Words at once true and kind,
Or not untrue and not unkind.

Philip Larkin

Bedside Readers

Bukowski is not my favorite bedside read.
I've known one too many men who keep
a troubling volume tucked beside the bed,
in their apartments at the razor edge
of Terror Street and Agony Way,
where they keep Love, the dog from Hell, at bay
and let no daylight penetrate that lair.

And Larkin, there's another to beware
between the sheets, for all I like his form.
This be the verse to keep us all forewarned.
A life with Larkin would have made me dive
straight off that rocky coastal shelf – Believe
me this – unless you want a timely end,
Don't read your lover 'Talking in Bed' in bed.

Diane Thiel

Infidelities

After he'd gone,
she found money in the sheets,
fallen when he pulled his trousers off.
Gathering the coins into a small pile
she set them on the window ledge.
They sat, gathering dust, guilt,
until one day her husband
scooped them into his pocket.
Small change for a call
he couldn't make from the house.

Moyra Donaldson

Since you're alike and lead a matching life,
Horrible husband and ill-natured wife,
Why all the discord and domestic strife?

Martial,
translated by James Mitchie

Life on Earth

When he came in
she gave him a flower
called 'Welcome Home Husband
However Drunk You Be'.

I am not drunk, he said;
this is not my home,
I am not your husband.

'Three mistakes
do not change the name of a flower'
she replied.

Ian McMillan

YOU JUST DON'T UNDERSTAND

So much time and therapy would be saved if all those tight-lipped conversations between couples that are ostensibly about doing the washing up, or what movie to go and see, or where to spend Christmas, came with subtitles, like the scene in *Annie Hall*. So instead of bickering tensely about whether to see *Son of Gladiator* the prequel, or a new French bittersweet comedy of childhood, you actually have that argument about spending too much time at work and get it out of the way. I think most men in a relationship will understand where Charles Bukowski is coming from in his poem 'wearing the collar' and they will identify with an exasperated D. H. Lawrence in his poem 'Intimates'. (And yet Lawrence's poem 'Gloire de Dijon' is one of the most contented love poems ever written . . . a reminder perhaps that men can be inconsistent too.)

Intimates

Don't you care for my love? she said bitterly.

I handed her the mirror, and said:
Please address these questions to the proper person!
Please make all requests to head-quarters!
In all matters of emotional importance
please approach the supreme authority direct! –
So I handed her the mirror.

D. H. Lawrence

He and She

When I am dead you'll find it hard,
    Said he,
To ever find another man
    Like me.

What makes you think, as I suppose
    You do,
I'd ever want another man
    Like you?

Eugene Fitch Ware

To His Mistress, Objecting to Him Neither Toying Nor Talking

You say I love not, 'cause I do not play
    Still with your curls, and kiss the time away.
    You blame me, too, because I can't devise
    Some sport to please those babies in your eyes; –
By Love's religion, I must here confess it,
    The most I love, when I the least express it.
    Small griefs find tongues; full casks are ever found
    To give, if any, yet but little sound.
Deep waters noiseless are; and this we know,
    That chiding streams betray small depth below.
    So when love speechless is, she doth express
    A depth in love, and that depth bottomless.
Now, since my love is tongueless, know me such,
    Who speak but little, 'cause I love so much.

Robert Herrick

wearing the collar

I live with a lady and four cats
and some days we all get
along.

some days I have trouble with
one of the
cats.

other days I have trouble with
two of the
cats.

other days,
three.

some days I have trouble with
all four of the
cats

and the
lady:

ten eyes looking at me
as if I was a dog.

Charles Bukowski

The More Loving One

Looking up at the stars, I know quite well
That, for all they care, I can go to hell,
But on earth indifference is the least
We have to dread from man or beast.

How should we like it were stars to burn
With a passion for us we could not return?
If equal affection cannot be,
Let the more loving one be me.

Admirer as I think I am
Of stars that do not give a damn,
I cannot, now I see them, say
I missed one terribly all day.

Were all stars to disappear or die,
I should learn to look at an empty sky
And feel its total dark sublime,
Though this might take me a little time.

W. H. Auden

WHEN LOVE CONGEALS . . .

'When love congeals/ It soon reveals/ The faint aroma of performing seals', sings Frank Sinatra in the Rogers and Hart song called, wait for it, 'I Wish I Was in Love Again'. Women can pick up the faintest whiff of a relationship going sour, while men need the full-on stench of decomposition to spot there might be a problem. The poems here cover all stages of the beginning of the end, from Maya Angelou's sad lyric 'Changing', through the sweaty 2 a.m. miseries of Anna Swir's poem to the graceful closure of Michael Drayton's 'The Parting'. One word of advice, if you turned to these poems first, before you go into full sniffer-dog mode, it is worth bearing in mind that there are such things as self-fulfilling prophecies.

The Bath Tub

As a bathtub lined with white porcelain,
When the hot water gives out or goes tepid,
So is the slow cooling of our chivalrous passion,
O my much praised but-not-altogether-satisfactory lady.

Ezra Pound

Changing

It occurs to me now,
I never see you smiling
anymore. Friends
praise your
humor rich, your phrases
turning on a thin
dime. For me your wit is honed
to killing sharpness.
But I never catch
you simply smiling, anymore.

Maya Angelou

Ending

The love we thought would never stop
now cools like a congealing chop.
The kisses that were hot as curry
are bird-pecks taken in a hurry.
The hands that held electric charges
now lie inert as four moored barges.
The feet that ran to meet a date
are running slow and running late.
The eyes that shone and seldom shut
are victims of a power cut.
The parts that then transmitted joy
are now reserved and cold and coy.
Romance, expected once to stay,
has left a note saying GONE AWAY.

Gavin Ewart

Fair to Say

It's fair to say you own a boat. It's yours.
Nothing luxurious. A rowing boat.
First it springs holes and then you lose the oars.
It's when the thing can barely stay afloat
Let alone speed you off to foreign shores –
At that point you no longer have a boat.

You rent a flat, a corrugated box,
No fancy furnishings, no welcome mat.
One day the landlord changes all the locks.
A dog moves in. It tries to kill your cat.
It's when the door stays closed, despite your knocks –
At that point you no longer have a flat.

You've got a boss. You've worked for him for years.
He is a firm, authoritative boss
Until one day the office disappears.
You ask him what to do. He's at a loss.
He looks away and covers up his ears –
At that point you no longer have a boss.

As for your man, the things he used to do
Like smile and speak, watch movies, make a plan,
Listen to music, kiss – to name a few –
He's given up, as if some kind of ban
Were on them all. When somebody who blew
Hot now blows cold and you've done all you can –
At that point you no longer have a man.

Sophie Hannah

Parting

Our love has been dying for years.
And now our parting
suddenly resurrects it.
Our love rises from the dead
uncanny
as a corpse which came to life in order to die
for the second time.

Every night we make love,
every hour we are parting,
every hour
we swear to each other faith till the grave.

We suffer intensively,
as one suffers in hell.
Each of us runs
a 110 fever.

Moaning out of hatred
we pluck our wedding photograph from the album
And every night till dawn,
crying, making love,
breaking into cold sweat,
we talk to each other,
we talk to each other,
we talk to each other,
for the first and the last time in life.

Anna Swir

The Parting

Since there's no help, come let us kiss and part;
Nay, I have done, you get no more of me,
And I am glad, yea, glad with all my heart,
That thus so cleanly I myself can free.
Shake hands for ever, cancel all our vows,
And when we meet at any time again,
Be it not seen in either of our brows
That we one jot of former love retain.
Now at the last gasp of Love's latest breath,
When, his pulse failing, Passion speechless lies,
When Faith is kneeling by his bed of death,
And innocence is closing up his eyes.
   Now if thou would'st, when all have given him over,
   From death to life thou might'st him yet recover.

Michael Drayton

AFTER HE'S GONE

Don't read these poems right away. I think in the first jagged days after the split you shouldn't be reading anything more demanding than labels in the off-licence. But when your nose has lost that swollen red tip, it is worth looking through this section. I think 'The Cost of Love' by the Australian poet Billy Marshall-Stoneking is compulsory reading for anyone going through the 'If only' stage. And at some point look on the bright side, the end of the affair is the only time in your life you will ever lose weight without trying,

He Said:

He said: I want you to be happy.
He said: I love you so.
Then he was gone.
For two days I was happy.
For two days, he loved me so.
After that, I was on my own.

Alice Walker

The Cost of Love

Maybe if she'd brushed her teeth before going to bed;
Maybe if she hadn't hung her stockings up in the bath;
Maybe if she'd faked orgasm more often;
Maybe if she hadn't put all her eggs in one basket;
Maybe if she'd gone for a guy with bad eyesight;
Maybe if she hadn't set her sights so high;
Maybe if she'd been blonde;
Maybe if she hadn't been so short;
Maybe if she'd been more realistic;
Maybe if she hadn't trusted men at all;
Maybe if she'd had a degree in business administration;
Maybe if she hadn't told him about her old boyfriends;
Maybe if she'd met him two years earlier;
Maybe if she'd had bigger tits;
Maybe if she hadn't tried so hard;
Maybe if she'd thought more about his feelings;
Maybe if he hadn't had an ex-wife;
Maybe if he hadn't been a musician;
Maybe if he hadn't been so shy;
Maybe if he had been younger;
Maybe if she'd been younger;
Maybe if he'd been a Catholic;
Maybe if she hadn't been Catholic;
Maybe, maybe . . .

Maybe if she'd let him tie her up;
Maybe if she'd set fire to herself;
Maybe if she would've died for him,
Just maybe . . . maybe
they might've still been together.

Billy Marshall-Stoneking

Ebb

I know what my heart is like
Since your love died:
It is like a hollow ledge
Holding a little pool
Left there by the tide,
A little tepid pool,
Drying inward from the edge.

Edna St Vincent Millay

Coat

Sometimes I have wanted
to throw you off
like a heavy coat.

Sometimes I have said
you would not let me
breathe or move.

But now that I am free
to choose light clothes
or none at all

I feel the cold
and all the time I think
how warm it used to be.

Vicki Feaver

You Died

You really died in me, not when
another gave me joy.
You died in me
when another gave me pain.

Anna Swir

FORGOTTEN BUT NOT FORGIVEN

In theory I think that closure is a very good thing and in theory there should be no reason why you can't still be friends, but in practice there is always one wound that never heals over completely. These are the poems for the days you feel inexplicably breathless with rage that the former object of your affections can still be walking around, unharmed. I think a little unworked-through hatred can be quite healthy, so long as you don't actually act on it.

at the antique sale
smiling at bargains she'd like
and won't know about

Frank Higgins

Years Later

　　　　when I see his writing on an envelope I think,
Oh yes! That was the man I married. I live
so easily without him now that I forget him
for months at a time. Until perhaps some man says
Let me help you.

　　　　　　And I knock his teeth out.

He mops up the blood, bewildered, and I apologise:
I'm so sorry. I just couldn't hear you for the echoes.

Let me help you. Let me do that for you.
You can trust me.

Dorothy Nimmo

MISSING YOU

These are the poems for when you have been separated from the one you love by life or death. I can't read Alun Lewis's poignant 'Postscript for Gweno' without the tears coming, for despite cynical comments earlier in this book, I can't believe there is a woman alive who doesn't want to be loved like that.

Postscript for Gweno

If I should go away,
Beloved, do not say
'He has forgotten me.'
For you abide,
A singing rib within my dreaming side;
You always stay.

And in the mad tormented valley
Where blood and hunger rally
And Death the wild beast is uncaught, untamed,
Our soul withstands the terror
And has its quiet honour
Among the glittering stars your voices named.

Alun Lewis

Joys that Sting

Oh doe not die, says Donne, *for I shall hate*
All women so. How false the sentence rings.
Women? But in a life made desolate
It is the joys once shared that have the stings.

To take the old walks alone, or not at all,
To order one pint where I ordered two,
To think of, and then not to make, the small
Time-honoured joke (senseless to all but you);

To laugh (oh, one'll laugh), to talk upon
Themes that we talked upon when you were there,
To make some poor pretence of going on,
Be kind to one's old friends, and seem to care,

While no one (O God) through the years will say
The simplest, common word in just your way.

C. S. Lewis

ACKNOWLEDGEMENTS

FLEUR ADCOCK: 'Excavations' from *Poems 1960–2000* (Bloodaxe Books, 2000), reprinted by permission of the publisher. MAYA ANGELOU: 'Poor Girl', 'They Went Home', 'Seven Women's Blessed Assurance', 'Come. And Be My Baby', and 'Changing' from *Complete Collected Poems* (Virago Press, 1994), reprinted by permission of Little, Brown & Company. MARGARET ATWOOD: 'Siren Song' from *Selected Poems 1965–1975* (Virago Press, 1975), reprinted by permission of Little, Brown & Company. W H AUDEN: 'The More Loving One' from *Collected Poems* (1976), reprinted by permission of the publishers, Faber & Faber Ltd. CONNIE BENSLEY: 'Metropolitan' from *The Back and The Front of It* (Bloodaxe Books, 2000), reprinted by permission of the publisher. ELIZABETH BISHOP: 'Casabianca' from *The Complete Poems: 1927–1979* (1983), reprinted by permission of the publishers, Farrar, Straus & Giroux, Inc. CHARLES BUKOWSKI: 'wearing the collar' from *You Get So Alone at Times That It Just Makes Sense*, copyright © Charles Bukowski 1986, reprinted by permission of the publisher, Black Sparrow Press. WENDY COPE: 'Going Too Far' and 'At 3 a.m.' from *Making Cocoa for Kingsley Amis* (1986); 'Bloody Men' and 'Advice to Young Women' from *Serious Concerns* (1992); 'Timekeeping' and 'Fireworks Poem' from *If I Don't Know* (2001); all reprinted by permission of the publishers, Faber & Faber Ltd. NOEL COWARD: 'I Am No Good at Love', reprinted by permission of Methuen Publishing Ltd. RUBY DEE: 'Marriage Counsel' from *My One Good Nerve* (Third World Press, 1998), reprinted by permission of the publisher. MOYRA DONALDSON: 'Infidelities' from *Snakeskin Stillettos* (Lagan Press, 1998); copyright holder not traced. GAVIN EWART: 'Ending' from *The Collected Ewart 1933–1980* (Hutchinson, 1980), reprinted by permission of Margo Ewart. VICKI FEAVER: 'Coat' from *Close Relatives* (Secker & Warburg, 1981), reprinted by permission of the author. ROBERT FROST: 'The Impulse' from *The Poetry of Robert Frost* edited by Edward Connery Lathem (Jonathan Cape, 1972), copyright © 1969 by Henry Holt & Co., reprinted by permission of The Random House Group Ltd on behalf of the Estate of Robert Frost, and Henry Holt & Company. ROBERT GRAVES: 'She Tells Her Love While Half Asleep' from *Complete Poems* (1997) reprinted by permission of the publishers, Carcanet Press Ltd. SOPHIE HANNAH: 'Hotels Like Houses', 'Slow it Right Down', and 'Fair to Say' from *Hotels Like Houses* (1996), reprinted by permission of the publishers, Carcanet Press Ltd. TONY HARRISON: 'Women All Cause Rue' after Palladas from *Palladas Poems: A Selection* (Anvil, 1975), copyright © Tony Harrison 1985, reprinted by permission of Gordon Dickerson. LANGSTON HUGHES: '50–50' from *Selected Poems* (Knopf, 1941) and 'Late Last Night' from *One Way Ticket* (Knopf, 1948), reprinted by permission of David Higham Associates. MICK IMLAH: 'Clio's' from *Birthmarks* (Chatto & Windus), reprinted by permission of The Random House Group Ltd. PHILIP LARKIN: 'Talking in Bed' and 'Administration' from *Collected Poems* (1990), reprinted by permission of the publishers, Faber & Faber Ltd. **JAMES LAUGHLIN**: 'O Best of All Nights, Return and Return Again' from *The Owl of Minerva: Poems* (Copper Canyon Press, 1987), reprinted by permission of New Directions Publishing Corporation. **ALUN LEWIS**: 'Postscript for Gweno' from *Raiders Dawn* (Allen & Unwin, 1942), reprinted by permission of Gweno Lewis. **C S LEWIS**: 'Joys that Sting' from *Poems* (Faber, 1964), reprinted by permission of the C S Lewis Company **LIZ LOCHHEAD**: 'Cowboys and Priests' and 'Telephone Song' from *True Confessions* (Polygon, 1985), copyright © Liz Lochhead 1985, reprinted by permission of the publisher. **CHRISTOPHER LOGUE**: 'Poem' from *Selected Poems*, reprinted by permission of the publishers, Faber & Faber Ltd. **IAN MCMILLAN**: 'Life on Earth' from *Selected Poems*, reprinted by permission of the publishers, Carcanet Press Ltd. **ANNE MCNAUGHTON**: 'Balls' first published in *Exquisite Corpse*, Vol 6, Nos 10–12, Oct-Dec 1988: copyright holder not traced. **LOUIS MACNEICE**: 'The Libertine' and lines from 'Trilogy for X' from *Collected Poems* edited by E R Dodds (Faber, 1966), reprinted by permission of David Higham Associates **CHRIS MANSELL**: 'Breakfast' from *Head, Heart, and Stone* (Fling Poetry, 1982), reprinted by permission of the author. **MARTIAL**: 'Since You're Alike . . .' from *Epigrams of Martial* translated by James Mitchie (Random House Inc, 1972), reprinted by permission of the publisher. **GLYN MAXWELL**: 'The Perfect Match' from *Out of the Rain* (Bloodaxe Books, 1992), copyright © Glyn Maxwell 1992, reprinted by permission of Gillon Aitken Associates Ltd. **ROBERT MEZEY**: 'A Thousand Chinese Dinners' from *Evening Wind* (University Press of New England, 1987), reprinted by permission of the author. **EDNA ST VINCENT MILLAY**: 'Ebb' and 'Oh, oh, you will be sorry for that word!' from *Collected Poems* (HarperCollins), copyright © 1921, 1923, 1948, 1951 by Edna St Vincent Millay and Norma Millay Ellis, reprinted by permission of Elizabeth Barnett, Literary executor. All rights reserved. **OGDEN NASH**: 'I Never Even Suggested It' and 'A Word to Husbands' from *Candy is Dandy: The Best of Ogden Nash* (Andre Deutsch, 2000), reprinted by permission of Carlton Books Ltd. **DOROTHY NIMMO**: 'Years Later' from *The Children's Game* (Smith/Doorstop, 1998), reprinted by permission of the Estate of Dorothy Nimmo. **FRANK O'CONNOR**: 'Advice to Lovers', copyright © Frank O'Connor, reprinted by permission of PFD on behalf of the Estate of Frank O'Connor **SHARON OLDS**: 'The Connoisseuse of Slugs' from *The Dead and The Living* (Alfred A Knopf, 1983), reprinted by permission of the publisher. **OODGEROO OF THE TRIBE NOONUCCAL**: 'Gifts' from *My People* (3e, The Jacaranda Press, 1990), reprinted by permission of John Wiley & Sons Australia. **DOROTHY PARKER**: 'General Review of the Sex Situation', 'On Being a Woman', and 'Ballade at Thirty-Five' from *The Collected Dorothy Parker* (1973), reprinted by permission of the publishers, Gerald Duckworth & Co. Ltd. **FELIX POLLAK**: 'The Dream' from *Subject to Change* (Juniper Press, 1978). **EZRA POUND**: 'The Bath Tub' from *Personae* (1909), reprinted by permission of the publishers, Faber & Faber Ltd. **ALEXANDER PUSHKIN**: 'She's gazing at you so tenderly' from *The Bronze Horseman* selected and translated by D M Thomas (Secker & Warburg, 1982), reprinted by permission of John Johnson Ltd. **VICKY RAYMOND**: 'Chat Show' from *Small Arms Practice* (Wm Heinemann, Australia, 1989), reprinted by permission of Curtis Brown (Aust) Pty Ltd on behalf of the author. **KENNETH REXROTH**: 'I Used to Tell You' from *Poems from the Greek Anthology* translated and edited by

Kenneth Rexroth (University of Michigan Press, Ann Arbor 1962), copyright 1962 by Kenneth Rexroth, reprinted by permission of the publisher. **ANNE SEXTON**: 'For My Lover, Returning to His Wife', reprinted by permission of Sterling Lord Literistic. **STEVIE SMITH**: 'I'll Have Your Heart' from *The Collected Poems of Stevie Smith* (Penguin), copyright © Stevie Smith 1972, reprinted by permission of the Executors of Stevie Smith. **JENNIFER STRAUSS**: 'What Women Want' from *Labour Ward* (Pariah Press, 1988). **WALLACE STEVENS**: 'Gray Room' from *Collected Poems* (1955), reprinted by permission of the publishers, Faber & Faber Ltd. **ANNE STEVENSON**: 'The Marriage' from *The Collected Poems: 1955–1995* (Bloodaxe Books, 2000), reprinted by permission of the publisher. **ANNA SWIR**: 'Parting' from *Happy as a Dog's Tail* (Harcourt, 1985), reprinted by permission of the publisher; and 'You Died' from *Fat Like the Sun* (The Women's Press, 1986), reprinted by permission of the translators, Margaret Marshment and Grazyua Baran. **SARA TEASDALE**: 'The Look', reprinted by permission of the Estate of Sara Teasdale. Diane Thiel: 'Bedside Readers' from *Echolocations* (Story Line Press, 2000), reprinted by permission of the author and Story Line Press (www.storylinepress.com). **ROSEMARY TONKS**: 'Story of a Hotel Room', copyright © Rosemary Tonks 1975, reprinted by permission of Sheil Land Associates. **ALICE WALKER**: 'He Said' from *Goodnight Willie Lee, I'll See You in the Morning* (The Women's Press, 1987), and 'Mississippi Winter IV' from *Horses Make a Landscape More Beautiful* (The Women's Press, 1985), reprinted by permission of David Higham Associates. **ANNA WICKHAM**: 'The Fired Pot' from *Memoirs and Notes* edited by R D Smith (Virago Press, 1984), reprinted by permission of Little, Brown & Company. **HUGO WILLIAMS**: 'Girl' from *Collected Poems* (2002), reprinted by permission of the publishers, Faber & Faber Ltd. **W B YEATS**: 'For Anne Gregory', 'The Folly of Being Comforted', and 'Aedh Wishes for the Cloths of Heaven' from *The Collected Poems of W B Yeats*, edited by Richard J Finneran (Macmillan, 1983), reprinted by permission of A P Watt Ltd on behalf of Michael B Yeats.

Although we have tried to trace and contact all copyright holders before publication, this has not been possible in every case. If notified the publisher will be pleased to make any necessary arrangements at the earliest opportunity.

INDEX